BRUNDIBAR

RETOLD BY TONY KUSHNER
PICTURES BY MAURICE SENDAK

AFTER THE OPERA BY HANS KRÁSA AND ADOLF HOFFMEISTER

BRUNDIBAR

MICHAEL DI CAPUA BOOKS/HYPERION BOOKS FOR CHILDREN

FOR CIARA AND ORLA   T.K.

FOR SUE KNUSSEN   M.S.

AND HE PUT HIS COLD, RED EAR ON MOMMY'S BREAST, AND SHE LOOKED UP AT THE CEILING, AND "HMMMM," THE DOCTOR SAID.

SO WE GRABBED A BUCKET AND WE RAN TO TOWN.

STRAIGHT INTO TOWN WE RAN, IT WAS A LONG TRIP, A HOT TRIP, BUT WE GOT THERE, AND THEY SAID:

AND WE DID, AND EVERYONE EVERYONE EVERYONE WAS THERE,
BUYING BUYING BUSY BUYING.

UNDER AN ICE-BLUE UMBRELLA AN ICE-CREAM SELLER SOLD
ICE-CREAM CONES, SINGING OUT:

MY ICE CREAM'S SO COLD IT BURNS!

GREEDY FOLK WHO GOBBLE HASTY

WILL TURN BLUE AND PUCKER-FACED-Y.

EAT IT SLOW, IT'S NICE AND TASTY!

VANILL-KOVA!

CHOCOLATE-KOVA!

CITRONOVA!

COLD-THROAT-KOVA!

CREAMY! DRIPPY! CHILLY! YUMMY!

PUT MY ICE CREAM IN YOUR TUMMY!

NEARBY A BAKER, HIS FACE LIKE A STICKY BUN, RAISIN EYES AND A
ROUND RED KNOB OF A NOSE, SHOOK HIS JELLY-JOWLS AND SANG:

FROM MY BAKERY, HOT AND STUFFY,
CRACKERS CRUNCHY, CREAM PUFFS PUFFY.
CORNBREAD, PUMPERNICKEL, RYE!
EVERY COOKIE, EVERY PIE,
EVERY BISCUIT, EVERY ROLL,
CROSS MY HEART AND HOPE TO DIE,
OVEN-FRESH, UPON MY SOUL!

FINALLY WE SAW HIM, HOORAY, THE MILKMAN! WITH HIS TALL
BOTTLES FULL OF FROTHY FRESH MILK, SINGING:

MILK, OH! MILK, OH! FARM-FRESH MILK, OH!
MILK FOR KIDDIES, MILK FOR MUDDERS,
MILK FOR CATS, FROM BESSIE'S UDDERS!
FRESH COLD MILK, OH, MILK, OH, MILK, OH,
BUTTER TOO, AND CHEESE.

WHERE DO KIDS GET MONEY? GROWN-UPS! NOW ALL AROUND US GROWN-UPS
WALKED AND THEIR MONEY SQURUNCHED AND TINKLED. BUT WE HAD NO
ICE CREAM TO SELL, NO CAKE TO SELL, NOT EVEN A SNAIL SHELL OR

A FINE SHINY PEBBLE TO SELL. AN EMPTY BUCKET WAS ALL WE HAD. BUT LOOK! WHERE? ACROSS THE SQUARE, THAT STRANGE CHARACTER THERE!

HIS HURDY-GURDY PHUMPHED AND WHEEZED AND THE SONG HE SANG WAS AWFUL! AWFUL! AWFUL! YOU WANTED TO STAY AWAY FROM HIM, ESPECIALLY IF YOU WERE SMALL, BUT THE GROWN-UPS FLUNG THEIR SHINY COINS AND SHOUTED "BRAVO, BRUNDIBAR!" BECAUSE BRUNDIBAR WAS, IN FACT, HIS NAME.

WHY DON'T WE SING? THEN PEOPLE WILL PAY US, COPPER CLINKING
IN OUR SOON-TO-BE-MILKBUCKET! A SONG OUR MOMMY TAUGHT US,
PERHAPS YOU KNOW IT?

WHEN THE WINTER WIND CAME BLO-O-W-ING
GOOSEY FLEW UP HIGH
DADDY HEARD HIS MOURNFUL HO-O-ONK-ING
WE HEARD DADDY CRY...

THOUGH WE SANG AS LOUD AS TWO SMALL KIDS CAN SING, WHO COULD HEAR US? BRUNDIBAR ACROSS THE SQUARE MADE SO MUCH NOISE NO ONE PAID US THE LEAST ATTENTION. THEY PAID US NO MONEY EITHER. AND ALL BECAUSE OF BELLOWING BRUNDIBAR.

WE HOPPED UP AND DOWN, WE WERE THAT MAD!

SO WE TWO BEARS LOPED ACROSS THE SQUARE AND
RAISED OUR PAWS HIGH IN THE AIR AND SHOOK
OUR BIG HEAVY BEAR BOTTOMS.

GRRRRRRRRRR

AND BRUNDIBAR CRANKED HIS HURDY-GURDY A MIGHTY CRANK, AND OH WHAT

A TEETH-CHATTERY BONE-RATTLEY HORRIBLE SONG HE HORRIBLY SANG!

HE SANG SO LOUD HIS EYES TURNED PINK AND YOU COULD SMELL THE
GARLIC HE ATE FOR BREAKFAST. DID WE MENTION HIS PURPLE FACE?
WE RAN AWAY, AND WHAT WOULD YOU DO? WE WERE FRIGHTENED!

YOU WOULD HAVE RUN TOO! WE HID IN AN ALLEY FULL OF OLD BOXES
AND CAST-OFF SHOES, AND WE CLOSED OUR EYES, AND MAYBE WE CRIED.
AND OUR VERY EMPTY BUCKET'S ROUND MOUTH SEEMED TO BE SAYING:

SUDDENLY—A SPARROW FLUTTERING FLAPPITY-FLAP! THE KIND YOU SEE IN BERRYBUSHES AFTER SNOW FALLS, BUT THIS SPARROW TALKED!

"RIGHT YOU ARE," HISSED A SILKY VOICE, A TALKING CAT! "CATS KNOW HOW IT FEELS TO HEAR: NO MILK FOR YOU, NOW SHOO, NOW SCAT!"

"BRUNDIBAR IS BIG," SAID A HANDSOME DOG. "AND YOU ARE SMALL,"
SAID THIS MOST SAGACIOUS ANIMAL.

AND STRAIGHTAWAY THE SPARROW FLIES, LEADING SCHOOLKIDS!
RAINCOATS! BOOKBAGS! LUNCHPAILS! TRAMP TRAMP TRAMP!

AND SO THE CHILDREN SANG:

MOMMY SINGS "ROCKABYE,
BABY, WHEN YOU ARE GROWN,
YOU'LL SING A LULLABY AND
I'LL BE LEFT ALONE.
BABY BLACKBIRD, FLY NOW.
TIME TO GO, WHO KNOWS WHY?
SPRING IS GONE, SUMMER'S IN,
WORLD AWAITS, IT'S TIME TO FLY."

TREES GROW HIGH, RIVERS DRY,
CLOUDS AND HOURS BILLOW BY,
DAY BY DAY, FLOWN AWAY . . .

BABY, IN SUCH A RUSH,

GREW UP, GREW STRAIGHT AND TALL.

MAYBE YOU'LL FEEL A BLUSH

WHEN, MOMMY, YOU RECALL

HOW YOU BATHED US NAKED

IN THE SINK, WARM AND WET,

GAVE US MILK, WHISPERED SOFT,

"LITTLE PET, YOU'LL SOON FORGET."

NOW YOU ARE VERY OLD.

YOUR HAIR IS SOFT AND GRAY.

MOMMY, THE CRADLE'S COLD,

BLACKBIRD HAS FLOWN AWAY.

COIN AFTER COIN AFTER COIN IS FLUNG INTO THE MARVELOUS WONDERFUL CHILDREN'S SOON-TO-BE-MILKBUCKET!

BRUNDIBAR RUNS CHASED BY CAT DOG SPARROW FOLLOWED BY

THREE HUNDRED AND TWO CHILDREN SHOUTING

FOLLOWED BY A THOUSAND GROWN-UPS SHOUTING

FOLLOWED BY A COP

FOLLOWED BY A VERY VERY VERY SMALL COCKROACH WHO HAS NOTHING TO DO WITH THIS STORY, BUT WHO WAS CURIOUS.

OH THUNDERY BLUNDERY BOTHERSOME BRUNDIBAR! SHALL YOU
BE POUNCED? AND WILL YOU BE TROUNCED? AND MUST YOU BE
THUMPED AND BUMPED AND SQUISHED AND VANQUISHED?
WELL, JUST ASK ANYONE, THEY'LL TELL YOU.

DOG CAT SPARROW SCHOOLKIDS CHEER!

EXIT, BRUNDIBAR, DISAPPEAR!

MILKMAN, HAVE YOU MILK TO SELL?

GREAT! AND HERE'S OUR MONEY, SIR.

MOMMY ISN'T FEELING WELL,

BUT WE'VE GOT LOTS OF MILK FOR HER!

REMEMBER, PLEASE BE BRAVE

AND BULLIES WILL BEHAVE!

They believe they've won the fight,
they believe I'm gone — not quite!

JULY 1942 – JULY 1944

Nothing ever works out neatly —
Bullies don't give up completely.
one departs, the next appears,
and we shall meet again, my dears!

though I go, I won't go far . . .
I'll be back. LOVE,
Brundibar